Jerem
Jo
bud.!
serve — heart, mind,
body & beard — er,
soul! Keep shining
Christ' love. Gratefully,
Jamie

prayer primer

morning or anytime prayers

david j. pedde

PRAYER PRIMER: Morning or Anytime Prayers

davidpedde.com

ISBN 978-0-9936641-2-0

Cover layout by Garrett D. Pedde

Cover art "Windows II"
Acrylic and charcoal on paper
©2016 Sunia Gibbs

CONTENTS

PRE-PRAYER

Some people say that prayer is a good idea because prayer changes things.

I prefer to say something like this:

Prayer is talking with God.

Talking with Him is a good idea.

God changes me.

God changes things.

Prayer changes me.

Pray, and let God worry.

~ Martin Luther

To be a Christian without prayer is no more possible than to be alive without breathing.

~ Martin Luther King, Jr.

Prayer does not change God, but it changes him who

prays.

~ Søren Kierkegaard

I have been driven many times to my knees by the overwhelming conviction that I had nowhere else to go.

~ Abraham Lincoln

God speaks in the silence of the heart.
Listening is the beginning of prayer.

~ Mother Teresa

Remember that you can pray anytime, anywhere.
Washing dishes, digging ditches, working in
the office, in the shop,
on the athletic field, even in prison
-- you can pray and know God hears!

~ Billy Graham

When we pray, the window of faith opens,
When we pray, all heaven stops to hear,
When we pray, a higher way is chosen,
When we pray, God is near.

~ David J. Pedde

TEACH ME TO PRAY

Prayer Journey

I am on a journey, a prayer journey. It is one that I've been on for most of thirty-five or forty years. Along the way, I've had many ups and downs to be sure. Times of desperation, boredom, fervency, neglect, and everything in between have each characterized this quest. Sometimes I have prayed obligatory prayers simply because I knew that it was "the right thing to do." I am a Christian leader, husband, and father after all, and praying is something that "a person in my position with my responsibilities" ought to do. Other times though, I have felt so completely starved for companionship or courage or answers, that I have been forcibly compelled to pray.

My experience is that genuine heart-to-heart communication with God is hard to start and then hard to stop. It requires diligence and patience. It takes time. It takes quiet. It takes me slowing down, quieting my heart and silencing my incessant self-talk long enough to hear His voice.

Depending on my immediate circumstances I have found my prayers ranging from the neatly academic to the desperately messy. They have been ordered, structured, and timed. They have been bombastic, scattered, even pathetic. Still, I pray. I pray because I want to know God.

He is my home.

How to use this book

I don't actually remember when it was that I started using a prayer journal nor exactly what motivated me to do so. I do know that when I started writing out my prayers for a number of reasons, it helped me to diarize my thoughts and my talks with God. When I would sense Him "stamping" part of His Word over my life, I would write it down as a reminder in order to seal it in my heart and my head. His Words have become etched in me over the years as I have daily recalled them, praying for myself and interceding for my family and others.

This is NOT intended as a book to read once and put down, but rather, for use in daily prayer. I have also designed it to be as interactive and customizable as possible.

Personalized Verses

Most of the verses have been written in the first person, personalized to be used in prayer, as prayers. That is how I pray them so that is how they are presented here. Each reference includes a link to the original version.

Add Your Own Verses/Prayers

At the end of each section of this book, there is a section entitled "*Personal Prayers.*" Write your own.

Lastly...

Linger. Take your time.

Listen. Prayer is a conversation between you and your Creator. What is He saying to you? Use the notes to write it down.

Try praying out loud. As in any dialogue, it is often helpful to hear yourself verbalizing your own thoughts and feelings.

Resist the temptation to "get through it" with a kind of checklist mentality. Pick up each day where you left off the day before or start fresh.

Read your Bible asking God to reveal Himself to you through its pages. Again, it is better to fully engage with a few verses than to hastily skim through chapter by chapter.

Enjoy the journey.

START HERE

Our Father in heaven,

Hallowed be Your Name.

Your kingdom come.

Your will be done

On earth as it is in heaven.

Give us this day our daily bread.

And forgive us our debts,

As we forgive our debtors.

And do not lead us into temptation,

But deliver us from the evil one.

For Yours is the kingdom and the power and the

glory forever.

Amen.

(Matthew 6:9-13 NKJV)

CHAPTER 1
HALLOWED BE YOUR NAME

Praying His Names

The notion of praying God's names was first introduced to me in a book I read in the late 1980's. I had been looking to give some structure to my prayers, not so dissimilar I suppose, to early followers of Christ who asked Him to teach them (how) to pray. Larry Lea, author of *Could You Not Tarry One Hour? Learning the Joy of Prayer*,[1] challenged Christians to pray "This Lord's Prayer," encouraging us to study and meditate on His Names in order to know Him

---

[1] Larry Lea, *Could You Not Tarry One Hour?: Learning the Joy of Prayer* (Lake Mary, FL: Charisma Media / Charisma House Book Group, 1987).

better. I determined to take up the challenge and have prayed this way ever since.

The following sections contain some of the Jehovah Names of God. Each section begins with a short poem/song (I sing these every day as a way of declaring my faith in God especially during times of difficulty or doubt) followed by brief reflections for meditation. Next come verses to use for prayer (in first person). Feel free to add your own verses and prayers as well.

Lord, I believe. Help my unbelief!

~ Father with a sick child
(Mark 9:23-24 NKJV)

Personal Prayers:

_____

_____

_____

_____

_____

_____

_____

_____

_____

_____

_____

_____

_____

_____

_____

_____

_____

_____

_____

_____

_____

_____

_____

HALLOWED BE YOUR NAME

JEHOVAH Tsidkenu (Savior)

> I believe in JEHOVAH Tsidkenu
> Righteousness is granted to me
> Forgiveness is mine through my Savior
> JEHOVAH Tsidkenu, I believe

You are my Sin Bearer, my Advocate, my Fall Guy, my Scapegoat, my Sovereign, my Owner, my King, and my God. You took my blame, erased my past, gave me a new identity and a new citizenship along with a new passport. I am made new.

You are my Love. I am Your beloved. You are my Master. I am Your servant. You are my Savior, the Source of my salvation. I cannot in any way save myself.

You died for me, I live for You. The debt I owe

You is unredeemable. I am and will remain, completely unable to pay it off. In truth, I belong to You. I have no rights. Although I deserve to be Your slave, You call me Your friend.

You knew no sin, no selfishness, yet You became sin for me, taking on the consequences of my selfishness.

You paid for my rebellion by Your piercing and my sins by Your crushing. You purchased my wholeness by Your beating and my healing by Your whipping. God made You Jesus, Who had no sin, to be sin for me, so that in You I might become the righteousness of God.

(II Corinthians 5:21 NIV*)

You were pierced for my rebellion, crushed for my sins. You were beaten so I could be whole. You were whipped so I could be healed. I have strayed away like a sheep. I have left Your paths to follow my own. Yet the Lord laid my sins on You.

(Isaiah 53:5-6 NLT*)

Yes, everything else is worthless when compared with the infinite value of knowing You, Christ Jesus my

Lord. For Your sake I have discarded everything else, counting it all as garbage, so that I could gain You Christ and become one with You. I no longer count on my own righteousness through obeying the law; rather, I become righteous through faith in You, Jesus Christ. For Your way of making me right with You depends on faith.

(Philippians 3:8-9 NLT*)

Personal Prayers:

_____

_____

_____

_____

_____

_____

_____

_____

_____

_____

_____

_____

_____

_____

_____

_____

_____

_____

_____

_____

_____

_____

_____

_____

_____

_____

_____

_____

HALLOWED BE YOUR NAME

JEHOVAH M'Kaddesh (Holiness)

> I believe in JEHOVAH M'Kaddesh
> Holiness is granted to me
> Sanctified, I'm free from sin's bondage
> JEHOVAH M'Kaddesh, I believe

You are my Holiness, in fact, my Owner. You are my Keeper and the Guardian of my heart. You make me clean. You keep me clean. I am forgiven. I am devoid of all guilt.

You sanctify me, setting me completely free by Your blood. You have every right to do so in that You have the keys to death and the grave, earning them at the cross.

I have no rights to my old sin, my selfishness, nor any of my old ways of doing things.

Every sinful act is an act of treason, duplicity, betrayal, and defiance against You my Creator, my Owner, my Savior and my Friend.

You are the Victor over sin. I thank You that I have been adopted into Your victory.

...if I confess my sins to You, You are faithful and just to forgive me my sins and to cleanse me from all wickedness.

(II Corinthians 5:21 NIV*)

For You saved me and called me to live a holy life. You did this, not because I deserved it, but because that was Your plan from before the beginning of time — to show me Your grace through Christ Jesus.

(2 Timothy 1:9 NLT*)

I will take a new grip with my tired hands and strengthen my weak knees. I will mark out a straight path for my feet so that those who are weak and lame will not fall but become strong. I will work at living in peace with everyone, and work at living a holy life, knowing that those who are not holy will not see the Lord.

(Hebrews.12:12-14 NLT*)

For I have sinned; I fall short of God's glorious standard. Yet You Father, with undeserved kindness, declare that I am righteous. You did this through Christ Jesus when You freed me from the penalty for my sins. For You presented Jesus as the sacrifice for my sin. I am made right with You when I believe that Jesus sacrificed His life, shedding His blood. This sacrifice shows that You were being fair when You held back and did not punish those who sinned in times past, for You were looking ahead and including me in what You would do in this present time. You did this to demonstrate Your righteousness, for You are fair and just, and You declare a sinner like me to be right in Your sight when I believe in Jesus.

(Romans 3:23-26 NLT*)

...if I have committed any sins, I will be forgiven. So I will confess my sins to another and we will pray for each other so that we may be healed. The earnest prayer of a righteous person has great power and produces wonderful results.

(James 5:15b-16 NLT*)

11

Personal Prayers:

_____

_____

_____

_____

_____

_____

_____

_____

_____

_____

_____

_____

_____

_____

_____

_____

_____

_____

_____

_____

_____

_____

_____

_____

_____

_____

_____

_____

_____

_____

_____

_____

_____

_____

_____

HALLOWED BE YOUR NAME

JEHOVAH Shalom (Peace)

> I believe in JEHOVAH Shalom
> His Spirit is granted to me
> Perfect peace beyond understanding
> JEHOVAH Shalom, I believe

You are my Calm and my Assurance.

You make things all right and give me hope that they will get better. As a result, I am quietly confident.

You give me peace beyond (exceeding abundantly above all I can ask or even imagine) my comprehension, beyond my circumstances. You are my calm in the midst of a storm, my safety in battle, my "everything is going to be OK." You give me hope for my todays and my tomorrows. I can hide, resting in Your great love.

You are the Counselor. I am the client. You guide me by the Holy Spirit into Your truth.

I will always be full of joy in the Lord - I will let everyone see that I am considerate in all I do, remembering that the Lord is coming soon. I won't worry about anything; instead, I'll pray about everything. I will tell God what I need, and thank Him for all He has done. Then I will experience God's peace, which exceeds anything I can understand. His peace will guard my heart and mind as I live in Christ Jesus. And now...one final thing. I will fix my thoughts on what is true, and honorable, and right, and pure, and lovely, and admirable. And I will think about things that are excellent and worthy of praise. I'll keep putting into practice all I learned and received ...Then the God of peace will be with me.

(Philippians 4:4-9 NLT*)

I can be sure that You, God will take care of everything I need. Your generosity is in the glory that pours from Jesus.

(Philippians 4:19 MSG*)

Now to You Who, by (in consequence of) the [action of Your] power that is at work within me, are able to [carry out Your purpose and] do superabundantly, far over and above all that I [dare] ask or think [infinitely beyond my highest prayers, desires, thoughts, hopes, or dreams] - To You be glory in the church and in You Christ Jesus throughout all generations forever and ever. Amen (so be it).

(Ephesians 3:20-21 AMP*)

For You know the thoughts that You think toward me ... thoughts of peace and not of evil, to give me a future and a hope. Then I will call upon You and go and pray to You, and You will listen to me. And I will seek You and find You, when I search for You with all my heart.

(Jeremiah 29:11-14a NKJV*)

Personal Prayers:

_____

_____

HALLOWED BE YOUR NAME

JEHOVAH Shammah (Presence)

> I believe in JEHOVAH Shammah
> His Presence is granted to me
> Holy Spirit, come dwell in this temple
> JEHOVAH Shammah, I believe

You are my Friend, my Companion, and my Confidant. I have intimacy with You Father God through Jesus Christ.

You are with me, so I am befriended. You are always with me. You know my every thought, see my every action.

Holy Spirit, You are an abiding (enduring, remaining, surviving, long-lasting, permanent, unshakable, steadfast) Presence in me.

As You sing over me and I join Your song,

I see (understand) and fear (worship) and trust (obey), as do those around me.

You are my Companion. I am Your chosen friend. May I live in constant awareness of Your presence.

You are with me and for me! What a gift!

My old self has been crucified with Christ. I no longer live, but Christ lives in me. So I live in this earthly body by trusting in You Son of God. You loved me and gave Yourself for me.

(Galatians 2:20 NLT*)

You are with me always, even unto the end of the age.

(Matthew 28:20b KJV*)

O Lord, You have examined my heart and know everything about me. You know when I sit down or stand up. You know my thoughts even when I'm far away. You see me when I travel and when I rest at home. You know everything I do. You know what I am going to say even before I say it, Lord. You go before me and follow me. You place your hand of blessing on my head. Such knowledge is too wonderful for me, too great for me to understand! I can never escape from your Spirit! I can never get away from your presence!

(Psalm 139:1-7 NLT)

I waited patiently for the Lord; And He inclined to me and heard my cry. He brought me up out of the pit of destruction, out of the miry clay. And He set my feet upon a rock making my footsteps firm. He put a new song in my mouth, a song of praise to our God; Many will see and fear and will trust in the Lord.

(Psalm 40:1-3 NASB)

Personal Prayers:

_____

_____

_____

_____

_____

_____

_____

_____

_____

_____

_____

_____

_____

_____

_____

_____

_____

_____

_____

_____

_____

_____

_____

_____

_____

HALLOWED BE YOUR NAME

JEHOVAH Rophe (Healing)

> I believe in JEHOVAH Rophe
> Healing is granted to me
> By His stripes, I have been healed
> JEHOVAH Rophe, I believe

You are my Healer, my Physician, my Caregiver, and my Personal Trainer.

You are the Great Physician. I am the patient.

You were beaten so I could be whole. You were whipped so I could be healed.

You take care of me, so I am healthy. You take care of each of the members of my family, so they are healthy.

You paid for my healing by personally enduring an unconscionable beating at the hands of Your accusers. You deserved none of it, took all of it, by actual stripes.

You endured man-inflicted sickness choosing illness, pain, and discomfort over wellness, wholeness, and comfort. You did it all on my behalf.

You are the Source and Sustainer of each breath I take, each perfectly aligned function of my body, every recognized and unrecognized, seen and unseen, move I make. I literally have my life in You.

You were pierced for my rebellion, crushed for my sins. You were beaten so I could be whole. You were whipped so I could be healed.

(Isaiah 53:5 NLT*)

Am I suffering? I will pray. Am I cheerful? I will sing psalms. Am I sick? I will call for the elders of the church, and let them pray over me, anointing me with oil in the Name of the Lord. And the prayer of faith will save me, and the Lord will raise me up. And if I have committed sins, I will be forgiven.

(James 5:13-15 NKJV*)

You Yourself bore my sins in Your body on the

cross, so that I might die to sin and live to righteousness; for by Your wounds I was healed. For I was continually straying like a sheep, but now I have returned to You, the Shepherd and Guardian of my soul.

(I Peter 2:24-25 NASB*)

Personal Prayers:

_____

_____

_____

_____

_____

_____

_____

_____

_____

_____

_____

HALLOWED BE YOUR NAME

JEHOVAH Jireh (Provision)

> I believe in JEHOVAH Jireh
> Provision is granted to me
> Daily bread, He's so graciously given
> JEHOVAH Jireh, I believe

You are my Supporter and my Benefactor.

You pay my way and give me wisdom regarding finances. You provide for me exceeding abundantly above all that I can ask or even imagine; I am cared for.

You give me everything I need. You are my Source.

You provide monetarily, enabling me and teaching me to be a wise manager of all of Your resources. As I do my part, that is, 100% obedience in all areas of my life, You physically bless me beyond my wildest comprehension.

First and foremost; You provide atonement for my sins by Your death, dear Lamb of God.

I know this: my God will also fill every need I have according to His glorious riches in Jesus the Anointed, our Liberating King.

(Philippians 4:19 VOICE*)

You instruct me not to worry about everyday life— whether I will have enough food and drink, or enough clothes to wear. Life is more than food, and my body is more than clothing. I will look at the birds. They don't plant or harvest or store food in barns, for my heavenly Father feeds them. And I am far more valuable to Him than they are. I cannot by all my worries add a single moment to my life. I repent of my little faith. I choose not to worry about these things, saying, 'What will I eat? What will I drink? What will I wear?' These things dominate the thoughts of unbelievers, but my heavenly Father already knows all my needs. I will seek the Kingdom of God above all else, and live righteously, and He will give me everything I need. I will not worry about tomorrow...

(Matthew 6:25-27, 30b-34a NLT*)

Every good and perfect gift is from above, coming down from the Father of the heavenly lights. You do not change like shifting shadows.

(James 1:17 NIV*)

I will bring all the tithes into Your storehouse knowing that You will open the windows of heaven for me. You will pour out a blessing so great that I won't have enough room to take it in! You've asked me to try it! I will put You to the test!

(Malachi 3:10 NLT*)

Personal Prayers:

_____

_____

_____

_____

_____

_____

_____

_____

_____

_____

_____

_____

_____

_____

_____

_____

_____

_____

_____

_____

_____

_____

_____

_____

_____

HALLOWED BE YOUR NAME

JEHOVAH Nissi (Protection)

> I believe in JEHOVAH Nissi
> Protection is granted to me
> We have refuge under Your banner
> JEHOVAH Nissi, I believe

You are my Protector and my Guardian.

You keep me, sustain me, protecting me from spiritual and physical evil.

You guard my heart and my mind with Your perfect peace. As I submit myself fully to You, the devil must flee from me.

You also provide a hedge of protection for those I am praying for today.

Finally, I will be strong in the Lord and in His mighty

power. I'm putting on the full armour of God so that
I can take my stand against the devil's schemes. For
my struggle is not against flesh and blood, but against
the rulers, against the authorities, against the powers
of this dark world, and against the spiritual forces of
evil in the heavenly realms. Therefore, I'm putting on
the full armor of God, so that when the day of evil
comes, I will be able to stand my ground, and after
I've done everything, to stand. I'm standing firm then,
with the belt of truth buckled around my waist, with
the breastplate of righteousness in place, and with my
feet fitted with the readiness that comes from the
gospel of peace. In addition to all this, I'm taking up
the shield of faith with which I can extinguish the
flaming arrows of the evil one. I'm taking the helmet
of salvation and the sword of the Spirit, which is the
Word of God. And I'm praying in the Spirit on all
occasions with all kinds of prayers and requests. With
this in mind, I will be alert and always keep on
praying for all the saints.

(Ephesians 6:10-18 NIV*)

Now all glory to You God. You are able to keep me
from falling away and will bring me with great joy into

31

Your glorious presence without a single fault. All glory to You. You alone are God, our Savior through Jesus Christ our Lord. All glory, majesty, power, and authority are Yours before all time, and in the present, and beyond all time! Amen.

(Jude 1:24-25 NLT*)

Personal Prayers:

_____

_____

_____

_____

_____

_____

_____

_____

_____

_____

_____

HALLOWED BE YOUR NAME

JEHOVAH Ro'i (Guide)

> I believe in JEHOVAH Ro'i
> Safe pasture is granted to me
> Where You lead me, my Shepherd, I will follow
> JEHOVAH Ro'i, I believe

YOU are my Shepherd, my Director, and my Boss.

You do the planning and patiently lead me step by step; I am led. You guide my way, knowing just exactly where I should go, what I should do.

You don't point me in one direction or another wishing me good luck, but rather, You guide me step by step, carrying me when I need You to.

In that You are my Good Shepherd, You even lay down Your own life to protect me and to ensure that I am able to make it to Your predestined destination for me.

You, Lord, are my Shepherd. I shall not want. You make me to lie down in green pastures; You lead me beside the still waters. You restore my soul; You lead me in the paths of righteousness for Your Name's sake. Yea, though I walk through the valley of the shadow of death, I will fear no evil; For You are with me; Your rod and Your staff, they comfort me. You prepare a table before me in the presence of my enemies; You anoint my head with oil; My cup runs over. Surely goodness and mercy shall follow me all the days of my life; And I will dwell in the house of the Lord forever.

(Psalm 23 NKJV*)

Personal Prayers:

_____

_____

_____

_____

_____

_____

_____

_____

_____

_____

_____

_____

_____

_____

_____

_____

_____

_____

_____

_____

_____

CHAPTER 2
YOUR KINGDOM COME, YOUR WILL BE DONE

...nevertheless, not my will but Yours be done.

~ Jesus Christ in the garden

Come Now, Your Kingdom

Be done, Your will

And by Your mercies

Please come and fill me

'Til the kingdoms of my heart

Bow to the Kingdom of the Christ

Your Kingdom come

Your will be done

When I don't see clearly

Help me to know Your face

When Your still voice bids me

I will come

When my feet grow weary

Help me to run this race I run

Words and Music by David J. Pedde
©1996 MAKERmusicMakers

I have been crucified with Christ. It is no longer I who live, but Christ Who lives in me. And the life which I now live in the flesh, I live by faith in the Son of God Who loved me and delivered Himself up for me.

(Galatians 2:20 NKJV)

I want to follow You. I realize that I must give up the things I want [deny myself; turn from selfishness; set aside my own interests]. I am willing even to give up my life to [take up my cross and] follow You.

(Matthew 16:24b EXB*)

Personal Prayers:

CHAPTER 3
OUR DAILY BREAD

I can be sure that God will take care of everything I need, His generosity...pours from Jesus.

> (Philippians 4:19 MSG*)

Whatever is good and perfect comes down to us from God our Father, who created all the lights in the heavens. He never changes or casts a shifting shadow.

> (James 1:17 NLT)

...Real religion, the kind that passes muster before God the Father, is this: Reach out to the homeless and loveless...

> (James 1:27 MSG)

I will be generous to the poor — I'll never go hungry...

> (Proverbs 28:27 MSG)

Personal Prayers:

_____

_____

_____

_____

_____

_____

_____

_____

_____

_____

_____

_____

_____

_____

_____

_____

_____

_____

_____

_____

_____

_____

_____

_____

_____

_____

_____

_____

_____

_____

_____

CHAPTER 4
FORGIVE US

Look on me with a heart of mercy, O God, according to Your generous love. According to Your great compassion, wipe out every consequence of my shameful crimes. Thoroughly wash me, inside and out, of all my crooked deeds. Cleanse me from my sins. For I am fully aware of all I have done wrong, and my guilt is there, staring me in the face. It was against You, only You, that I sinned, for I have done what You say is wrong, right before Your eyes. So when You speak, You are in the right. When You judge, Your judgments are pure and true. For I was guilty from the day I was born, a sinner from the time my mother became pregnant with me. But still, You long to enthrone truth throughout my being; in unseen places deep within me, You show me wisdom. Cleanse me of my wickedness with hyssop, and I will be clean. If You wash me, I will be whiter than snow. Help me hear joy and happiness as my accompaniment, so my bones, which You have broken, will dance in delight instead. Cover Your face so You will not see my sins, and erase my guilt from the record. Create in me a clean heart, O God; restore within me a sense of being brand new. Do not throw me far away from Your presence, and do not remove Your Holy Spirit from me. Give back to me the deep delight of being saved by You; let Your willing Spirit sustain me. If You do, I promise to teach rebels Your ways and help sinners find their way back to You...You don't take pleasure in sacrifices or burnt offerings. What sacrifice I can offer You is my broken spirit because a broken spirit, O God, a heart that honestly regrets the past, You won't detest.

(Psalm 51:1-13, 16b,17 VOICE)

Make Me New / Make in Me a Clean Heart

Make me new like an early spring rain
Make me new, make me new

Change my heart, revive me again

Make me new, make me new

Make me new like the dawning of day

Make me new, make me new

Transform my mind, renew me again

Make me new, make me new

I confess that I am in a mess

I need Your righteousness

Make in me a clean heart

Wash away my selfish stains

That I might sing Your praise

Make in me a clean heart

Against You only, I've sinned

Still mercy beckons me to enter in

Holy, holy, holy

Words and Music by David J. Pedde
©1996 MAKERmusicMakers

Personal Prayers:

_____

_____

CHAPTER 5
LEAD US, DELIVER US

I will be careful how I walk, not as an unwise person
but as a wise one making the most of my time,
because the days are evil. So then, I will not be
foolish, but understand what the will of the Lord is.

(Ephesians 5:15-17 NASB*)

I love Thee, o Lord, my Strength. The Lord is my
Rock and my Fortress and my Deliverer. My God, my
Rock, in Whom I take refuge; my Shield and the
Horn of my salvation, my Stronghold. I will call upon
the Lord, Who is worthy to be praised. And I am
saved from my enemies.

(Psalm 18:1-3 NASB*)

The Lord is my shepherd; I shall not want. He makes
me to lie down in green pastures; He leads me beside
the still waters. He restores my soul; He leads me in

the paths of righteousness for His name's sake. Yea, though I walk through the valley of the shadow of death, I will fear no evil; For You are with me; Your rod and Your staff, they comfort me. You prepare a table before me in the presence of my enemies; You anoint my head with oil; My cup runs over. Surely goodness and mercy shall follow me all the days of my life; And I will dwell in the house of the Lord forever.

(Psalm 23:1-6 NKJV)

Personal Prayers:

_____

_____

_____

_____

_____

_____

_____

_____

CHAPTER 6
YOURS IS THE KINGDOM, POWER, AND GLORY

We Enthrone You

To the glory of God the Father
To the glory of God the Son
To the glory of God the Spirit
To the glory of God, Three in one

We enthrone You with our praises
We enthrone You in our lives
We enthrone You, King of the ages,
We enthrone You, You are Christ

Words and Music by David J. Pedde
©1996 MAKERmusicMakers

Personal Prayers:

_____

_____

_____

_____

_____

_____

_____

_____

_____

_____

_____

_____

_____

_____

PRAY WITHOUT CEASING

...I'll pray all the time

(I Thessalonians 5:17 MSG*)

I'll never stop praying

(I Thessalonians 5:17 NLT*)

...I'll pray wherever I am...

(I Timothy 2:8 VOICE*)

Prayer does not fit us for the greater work; prayer is

the greater work.

~ Oswald Chambers

Do not make prayer a monologue - make it a

conversation.

~ Unknown

Personal Prayers:

_____

_____

_____

_____

_____

_____

_____

_____

_____

_____

_____

_____

_____

_____

_____

_____

_____

_____

ENJOY THE JOURNEY

Prayer Journey

The call to prayer is simply an invitation to talk with God. He initiates. We respond. He calls. We answer. He bids. We come.

You can be sure of this. He wants to talk, He wants to listen. So listen. Talk. Start slowly but keep at it.

Enjoy the journey.

It seems that God is clearly calling His people everywhere to prayer, and as Matthew Henry said generations ago, "Whenever God is preparing to do something great in the earth, He first sets His people a-praying!

~ Dick Eastman

Heaven is full of answers to prayer for which no one

bothered to ask.

~ Billy Graham

Prayer...the key of the day and the lock of the night.

~ George Herbert

Pray wherever you are.

Reach your holy hands to heaven—without rage or

conflict—completely open.

~ Apostle Paul

ABOUT THE AUTHOR

david.j.pedde | your.worship.mentor

worship leader | songwriter | producer | educator | coach | consultant | author

...helping worship leaders and pastors rethink what they do and redo what they think...

Dave has been involved in worship ministries for 40 years, although he doesn't really want anyone to believe he is that old. Originally from Edmonton, Alberta, he has served as a worship pastor in 7 churches in Canada and the U.S. and worked as Composer in Residence at North Central University in Minneapolis for 18 years where worship and songwriting were among his academic specialties.

He frequently travels as a featured speaker, worship leader, teacher, and coach, and has extensive studio experience having produced 32 or so albums to date. Dave has over 100 published songs, with his most recent recordings being Windows Volume One and The Planting.

Dave earned his Masters degree from The Robert E. Webber Institute for Worship Studies and has served as Founder and President of Sanctus School for Worshippers.

Dave and Debbie have been married 36 years and have five children. He likes coffee, baseball and mornings...

Made in USA - Kendallville, IN
1063777_9780993664120
03.27.2020 0754